Go Read

Published by The Trevor Romain Company
Austin, TX
www.trevorromain.com

ISBN: 978-1-64339-973-7

Printed in the United States of America

Dedicated to the kids
at the Botshabelo Orphanage

Hello!

I am a book.

Thank you for
opening my cover and
coming in for a visit.

Let me tell you a little about myself.

I do not need batteries or a charger to work.

Unless of course you are using a flashlight to read me under the covers. The flashlight itself will need batteries, but not me.

You should ask a grown-up to read under the covers with you sometime...it's really fun!

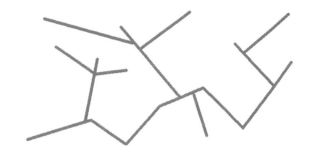

If you drop me I will not crack.

If you sit on me I will not break;
I will only make you a little taller.

I have twenty-six roommates who live in this book with me. I am their manager. They are an interesting bunch. They call themselves the Alphabet.

Here they are in alphabetical order.

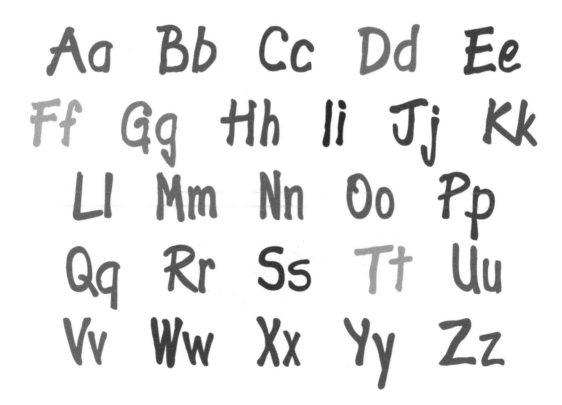

When I first met the alphabet I would forget how to say their names. So my friend, who created me, drew some fun ways to help me remember.

Let me introduce them all to you:

A is for an alligator eating apple pie.

Bb

B is for a blue bear bouncing in the bath.

C is for a circus clown juggling on a cow.

Dd

D is for a dog drawing with a duckling.

Ee

E is for an elephant eating scrambled eggs.

F is for a frog floating on a fish.

Gg

G is for a goofy giggling gorilla.

Hh

H is for a happy hen wearing a hat.

I is for an Ibis standing on an igloo.

J is for a jellyfish sitting on a jack-o'-lantern.

K is for a kangaroo playing a kazoo.

L l

L is for a lion licking a lollipop.

M is for a mouse eating a muffin.

Nn

N is for a narwhal wearing a necktie.

O is for an owl reading an orange book.

P p

P is for a pig painting a pretty picture.

Qq

Q is for quiet so I can't say anymore.

Rr

R is for a rhino running in the rain.

Ss

S is for a snake studying at school.

T is for a tortoise walking on a tightrope.

Uu

U is for up and also for under.

Vv

V is for vegetables from Victor the farmer.

Ww

W is for a whale wearing a wig.

X is for a xylophone and other words
that are hard to say like Xhosa and xenops.

Y is for a yellow jacket,
so you'd better turn this page quickly!

Z is for a zero that's why there is nothing on this page.

a b c d e f g h i j k l m n o p q r s t u v w x y z

I hope you enjoyed meeting the alphabet.
I know they enjoyed meeting you.

If you don't want to forget their names,
practice saying them out loud.

Psssst. Here's a secret. Making friends with the
alphabet, and remembering their names, will make
you a great reader!

Thank you so much for reading me cover to cover.
You are welcome back anytime!

Books sometimes get lonely sitting unopened in a pile or on a shelf, so come back and visit me again soon.

And remember, if you want to make a book, or yourself, very happy...

GO READ!